Raj Kapoor

The Great Showman

Published in 2003 by

Rupa & Co

7/16, Ansari Road, Daryaganj
New Delhi 110 002

Sales Centres:
Allahabad Bangalore Chandigarh Chennai
Dehradun Hyderabad Jaipur Kathmandu
Kolkata Ludhiana Mumbai Pune

Cover & Book Design by
Arrt Creations
45 Nehru Apts, Kalkaji, New Delhi 110 019

Printed in India by
International Print-O-Pac Ltd.
B204-205, Okhla Ind. Area, Phase-I,
New Delhi-20

Raj Kapoor

The Great Showman

Lata Khubchandani

Rupa & Co

CONTENTS

Mera Naam Raj Kapoor

Who was Raj Kapoor? Should he be defined through his work? Or his personality? As the man? The actor? Or the filmmaker?

Was he the Charlie Chaplin of India? The founder of RK Films or just Raju, the common man who traipsed all over the silver screen and into the hearts of millions?

Raj Kapoor was all this and more. He was the great showman. Though he directed just about a dozen films and acted in about 65 films during his 40-year career, he won himself the undisputed title of the greatest showman of our times.

His films are aired repeatedly, and his work has been analysed, eulogised, criticised. He did not have the depth to portray reality like a Satyajit Ray or even a Guru Dutt. Nor the Bimal Roy touch of searing your soul through issue based films. Nor the sense of high drama like Mehboob Khan. Yet Raj Kapoor emerged as the supreme entertainer among his peers.

Sharing the sidewalk...

His films were mega blockbusters, had memorable songs, magnificient themes and glorified the common man. They were pure and simple entertainment — commercial, reaching out to both the front benchers and the elite. His speciality was to touch that chord which the masses and the classes had in common. He had a burning need to cross the boundaries of divisiveness and unite people through the bonds of love. Perhaps, in exposing this common bond that links every man, Raj Kapoor's films served their greatest purpose — as a uniting force in as diverse a country as India.

Little wonder then, that his name is familiar to every Indian. And is even well-known abroad as Raj Kapoor was not only an actor/ filmmaker, but also ended up being India's cultural ambassador, particularly in Russia and the Arab countries. There he was almost better known and better loved than our politicians. Ironical, because it was his romanticised social themes that touched the heart of the denizens behind the iron curtain.

Raj Kapoor's personality too expressed a benign affection, particularly towards people whose lives he touched in any way. He was a giver in more than the overt sense; and even with people who he wanted to use, he ended up giving, more than taking. He once said, "People have often cheated me, used me, thinking that they're making a fool out of me, little knowing that I am aware of what is happening and have willingly let myself be made a fool of."

Once Rashid Khan, a character actor and a Dev Anand (Navketan) campwallah needed some money to invest in a small business. After being refused by the Anands, he approached Raj Kapoor, who had never used him in any film (those were the days of

At the premiere of Shree 420 *in 1955, with wife Krishna and Nargis in Calcutta*

camp loyalists and the supporting cast and crew always remained the same in most films). Raj Kapoor heard him out and at once ordered an assistant to give him the money. When the man started thanking him, he said, "Don't worry, consider it an advance, I'll use you in a film sometime!"

Dilip Kumar, Raj Kapoor and Dev Anand with the then Prime Minister of India Jawaharlal Nehru, 1968

Yet the same Raj Kapoor could snub a socialite who sidled up to him at a party smoking a cigarette saying, "Brazenness doesn't become a woman!"

This attitude towards 'woman' remained consistent throughout his life. The Kapoor men have taken liberties galore but the Kapoor women were kept under a protective *purdah* at home. Hypocritical? No – just the Kapoor tradition which had it's own charm.

Chapter One

Early Years

(Born 14th December 1924 — died 2nd June 1988)

Ranbir Raj Kapoor, like many pre-partition Indians, was born in Pakistan, in Peshawar, to Prithviraj Kapoor and Ramsarni Kapoor. Few know that apart from the flamboyant Shammi Kapoor and the charming Shashi Kapoor, Raj Kapoor had two more brothers, Virendra and Devendra, who died early. They have one sister, Urmila.

As a kid Raj Kapoor had three petnames. They called him Chisto also Gora, and sometimes Lashkaree.

Raj Kapoor's parents migrated to Mumbai in 1927. While Prithiviraj Kapoor was looking for work and doing small roles to keep the home fires burning, the young Raj Kapoor, completely disinterested in studies, became increasingly fascinated by films. He also started getting spoilt, was self-indulgent, loved eating and hated studying.

Recalls brother Shammi Kapoor, "Rajji had a cupboard in his room which was always kept locked. No one dared to open it. I always wanted to know what was inside. Once I got the chance to open it and guess what I found? Innumerable stacks of magazines, cuttings, posters, dress designs — everything to do with costumes, set designing, Hollywood filmstars and the like. He had been meticulously collecting this stuff for years and storing it like invaluable treasure."

This was Raj Kapoor preparing to be a filmmaker. He had managed to reach the matriculation level, but failed the preliminary examination. Papa Prithviraj took this lightly enough saying, "Oh! well there's always next time."

Raj Kapoor then announced his intention of not appearing for the exams again. He explained, "Papaji, when a boy wants to become a doctor, he goes to medical college, when he wants to become a

Prithviraj and Raj Kapoor together in the 1946 release Valmiki

lawyer he goes to law college. I want to make movies, be a director, a producer, an actor. And instead of wasting five years studying something I don't want to learn and joining a studio finally, I'd like to start work in a studio at once."

A worried Papa Prithviraj confided his anxiety to friend Kidar Sharma, who offered to take the boy under his wing. But there were conditions — Raj had to start on the lowest rung and work his way up. Nor was Prithviraj allowed to interfere in his son's training.

Raj Kapoor with mentor Kidar Sharma

"Prithvi agreed," recalled Sharma, "and Raj Kapoor came in as a third assistant, as a clapper boy, in my production house. I noticed that he was very taken with his looks. Even though his job was just to give the clap, he'd make it a point to find out how far he needed to be from the camera in order to get a close-up of himself. (Raj Kapoor later admitted that the cameraman and he had a pact that he'd take a close-up of him and give him the photo) He'd watch the camera eagerly and if there was an opportunity to get in front of it, he took it. Each time he had to give the clap, he'd quickly comb his hair, steal a glance in the mirror and only when he was satisfied with what he saw, would he come and sound the clapper board.

"I noticed this but attributed it to the vagaries of youth and let it pass. But one day I needed to take a shot of the setting sun and we had lost precious days because the weather had been playing up. I called Raj and told him, 'Look son, promise me two things today. When I shoot these scenes, do not comb your hair or preen yourself before the mirror. I cannot afford to lose another day.' Raj promised he wouldn't.

"It was a scene where an old king was to be shown at the end of his life and the ebbing sun was to symbolise this. As soon as we were ready, Raj forgot his promise and went to comb his hair. Then, flustered, he came so close to the king and sounded the clap, that the king's beard got caught in the board and we had to cut the shot.

"I was furious and slapped Raj Kapoor hard. He was so fair that my finger marks showed up on his face immediately. But he didn't say a word. I went home that night and just couldn't sleep. Had I been unfair to the boy? After all, I wasn't paying him anything. He

In Prithvi Theatres' stage play Pathan *(1947-48)*

had a right to be resentful. He was the son of the well-known Prithviraj Kapoor.

"Then, I made up my mind. Next morning as soon as Raj Kapoor arrived I called him to my room. He came in smiling and said, 'Do you want to make these finger marks on my other cheek also?' I said, 'No son' and gave him a cheque for Rs. 5000/- and told him that he would be the hero of my next film, *Neel Kamal* (1944). He looked surprised and said, 'No, don't cast me. I am too fat, your film will fail.' But I had realised after my sleepless night that this boy craved to be in front of the camera." The film was made with a 19-year-old Raj Kapoor and a 13-year-old Madhubala (her first film)"

Raj Kapoor and Madhubala in Neel Kamal

The film became a big hit.It was technically Raj Kapoor's first film, though he had done bit roles as a child artiste in films like *Inquilab* in 1935 (Debaki Bose) and in plays such as 'The Toy Cart'. After that it did not take too long for the actor to conceptualise films for himself and at the age of 23, he came up with his first film — *Aag* (1948). This was the birth of Raj Kapoor the director, producer and actor all rolled into one.

Chapter Two

Coming Into His Own

As a filmmaker, Raj Kapoor was never young. He was neither hesitant nor an amateur. Even to his first film *Aag,* he brought an experience which may have been simmering in his brain long before he actually took up the director's baton. He knew what he wanted and executed it to his satisfaction.

In *Aag,* he dealt with the idealistic but subjective theme of a man who is in love with theatre, and explores his relationships with three women while on this idealistic trip. The film also revealed

Raj's tendency to pick up real-life incidents and situations and dramatise them, make them larger than life for his celluloid dreams.

The famous confrontation scene between father and son in *Aag*, is a take off on his real life showdown with Prithviraj, when he announced his intention of quitting school midway. This real life translation into reel life was seen over and over again in his films, most notably in *Bobby*, where Dimple the leading lady is introduced to Rishi Kapoor with *besan* (gram flour) on her forehead and hands. This is how Raj Kapoor himself had first met Nargis.

With Nargis in Awara

After *Aag* and before his own second production *Barsaat*, audiences saw him in a love triangle with Dilip Kumar and Nargis — in Mehboob Khan's *Andaz*. This film was a box office wonder and for *Barsaat*, Raj Kapoor cast Nargis opposite himself. In *Barsaat* he was delicately suggesting that the rural woman is so much purer than the urban, educated but more brazen female.

Barsaat had a musical score which remains immensely popular half a century after it was composed. The film was a pure and clear romance, and also provided Raj Kapoor with the emblem that adorned all RK Films. Raj Kapoor froze the shot where he's playing the violin and Nargis comes running into his arms. He holds his violin in one hand and his lady in the other. This utterly imaginative picture, however, had to be replaced after Nargis' marriage to Sunil Dutt.

Barsaat also entrenched Lata Mangeshkar in the RK fold forever thereafter. Songs like *'Jiya beqarar hai....', 'Hawa mein udta jaaye'* and *'Humse mile tum barsaat mein'* even while they were being

Prem Nath and Nimmi in Barsaat

recorded suggested to those present, that history was being created. *Barsaat* was another big triumph for Raj Kapoor.

Raj finalised Nimmi for a role in *Barsaat*, while he was working in *Andaz*. Nimmi was a shy, tongue-tied teenager, visiting the set as Mehboob Khan's guest. Remembers Nimmi reflectively, "I was sitting next to Nargis' mother when Raj Kapoor walked up to her to pay his respects. He asked me my name, but I was so shy that I could hardly reply. He was looking for a totally new and innocent face to introduce in *Barsaat*, and had rejected everybody he had met. My shyness seemed to do the trick. He requested Mrs. Mehboob Khan to ask my grandmother for permission to cast me in his film.

"I was so nervous during the screen test that, though I had learnt my dialogues, I started sobbing as I said them. But Raj Kapoor was very happy and signed me on. He realised that I was new and frightened by this unfamiliar atmosphere. So the first thing he did, was to make me tie a *raakhi* on him saying, 'From today, you are my sister, you own this studio and can be comfortable here.'"

CHAPTER THREE

Establishing R K Studios

Once Raj Kapoor had tasted success after producing and directing *Aag*, there was no looking back for him. His imagination soared the heights of fancy and he lived, ate and breathed cinema. He also began realising the need to create his own cinematic environment around him. These were the birth pangs of Raj Kapoor the studio owner and film magnate. He wanted to make films at his own pace without being subservient to studio shifts and fluctuating finances. For this he required infrastructure, a studio of his own.

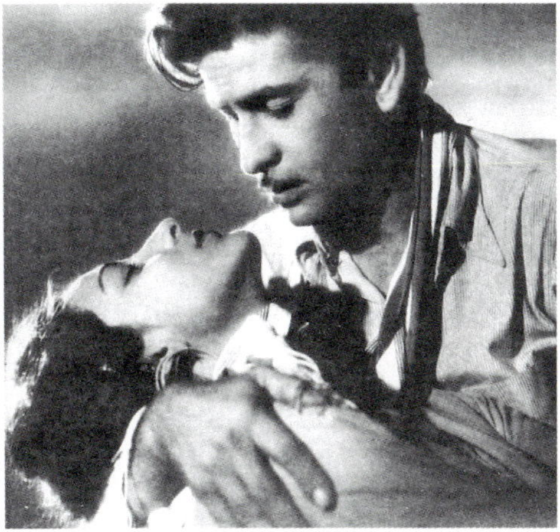

The still from Barsaat, *which was later frozen into the RK emblem*

For a start, he bought the first RK office at Famous Studios in Mahalaxmi in 1948, the same year in which *Aag* was released. In 1950, he set up RK Studios at Chembur, and this coincided with the making of *Awara.* He also set up a production team which remained with him throughout his life. This consisted of cinematographer Radhu Karmarkar, storywriters K.A. Abbas and V.P. Sathe, the nationalist-socialist lyric writer Shailendra, the romantic lyricist Hasrat Jaipuri, the composer duo Shanker-Jaikishan, and playback singer Mukesh who also became Raj Kapoor's alter ego.

Raj Kapoor with Hasrat Jaipuri, Jaikishen, Shankar and Shailendra, 1960

He called Mukesh his "soul" and his lyricists, composers and music team his "heart". He claimed that without them he was nothing. And, of course, there was Lata Mangeshkar, who became a permanent part of his musical genius. So inspired was he by her voice and persona, that he wrote *Satyam, Shivam, Sundaram* with her in mind.

Each film that rolled out of RK Studios was a movement ahead from the last. And his production house, RK Productions, became a revered name, to be pronounced in hushed tones. It was everybody's dream to be part of an RK film. Just like the inimitable New Theatres of yore, RK Productions commanded the respect of both cinegoers and artistes with its trademark romances, musicals and films based on social themes.

Zeenat Aman in Satyam Shivam Sundaram

Chapter Four

The Birth of the Tramp

Raj Kapoor's third magnum opus was *Awara.* This movie played a very important role in his career, as it gave birth to the quintessential Raj Kapoor persona, which he is best remembered by even today.

Awara was responsible for many firsts in Raj Kapoor's life. He got into attire, which was to remain with him throughout his life; rolled-up trousers, hat, torn shoes and the Chaplinesque tramp was born. Raj had been strongly influenced by Charlie Chaplin's ideas and characters and it was from *Awara* that the Indian Chaplin came into being. The character remained throughout Raj Kapoor's films till his death.

Ironically, apart from the birth of the lovable tramp, *Awara* also marked the beginning of Raj Kapoor's flirtation with the spectacular, of his magnificent showmanship. The film had the most amazing song picturisations, which are still cited as landmarks. The dream sequence in *'Ghar aaya mera pardesi, pyas bujhi meri akhiyan ki.....'* took three months and exorbitant amounts of money to picturise. It was elaborately shot, on thirteen sets, choreographed by Madame Simki and seduced the imagination of viewers everywhere.

It is said that RK Studios was not even fully built but the sets for *Awara* were created by his art director M.R. Achrekar on an entire floor. This song, which lasted nine minutes on screen, played an important role in helping the hero to arrive at a moral decision for resolving the dilemma he was facing. This was song picturisation at its creative best.

Raj Kapoor's relationship with Nargis had already been established in films like *Aag, Barsaat* and *Andaz*. The reel life love spilled over into their personal life and *Awara* gave ample proof of the compulsiveness of their love. The screen came alive when the two appeared together and no one could fail to notice their comfortable intimacy. Raj's romanticism, his intense love scenes and his imaginative picturisation of them, thrilled the audiences.

The couple became a rage. Nargis became an essential part of the RK establishment. Raj Kapoor later said, "The RK emblem is a reflection of her contribution to the studio. RK *ke har set mein Nargis ki mehnat aur lagan chhupi hui hai.*"

Awara also entrenched Raj Kapoor and Nargis in the hearts of the audiences everywhere, particularly in Russia. Though it was released in 1952 in India,

With Nargis in Shree 420

it was shown in the USSR in 1954 as *Brodigaya.* It became a hit overnight. They dubbed the film in various languages. Even the songs were translated into different languages and sung on the streets by the people.

Satyajit Ray's *Pather Panchali* was also released in 1954. Apparently, when Raj Kapoor saw the movie, he was dumbfounded and wanted Ray to direct a film for RK Productions. But Ray refused saying that he was not comfortable with the Hindi language. But just as *Pather Panchali* became a classic with the elite, *Awara* became a classic with the common man. Its very basic ideas, its vociferous tirades against the imbalances in society and the moral decadence around, appealed to all. This was Raj Kapoor, the entertainer at his most expressive. He never made his audiences jump intellectual hoops to understand his cinematic idiom. It was overt and obvious — always easily understood.

With Satyajit Ray in 1966

CHAPTER FIVE

The Social Reformer

What is Raj Kapoor's precise contribution to films? He saw his protagonist as an *ingénue*. His Raju (played by himself) was always forced into wrong-doing or was an innocent victim of society's wrong attitudes. Yet his sheer innocence, exuberance, optimism and inherent goodness as it were, gave him simple joy in the smallest pleasures of life. Too simplistic, one might say, and could be carried too far at times. But it was an appropriate vehicle for what he was trying to convey and it worked with the masses.

In *Shri 420*, he explored the dilemma of the common man. The title suggested that the hero is forced to become a gentleman conman because society does not allow honest men a living. This film was definitely a progression over *Awara* and more complex in its treatment. If *Awara* showed the hero as a simpleton, in *Shri 420* he was an educated youth, looking for work till he discovers it is easier to make money if he is not carrying the baggage of values and principles.

But Raj Kapoor's penchant for seeing even real issues through the pink-tinted glasses of sentimentality gave this film too a resolution which culminated in an emotional 'all's well that ends well'. His hero even after deciding on a life of 'easy money' still has a heart of gold. The song *'Mera joota hai Japani'* shouted this out for all to hear. Nobody was to conclude that the protagonist was past redemption even though he does have lapses as expressed in the song *'Mud mud ke na dekh mud mud ke'*.

This '420' was adorable — his friendship with the pavement dwellers, his sense of belonging to an environment where the street dog and the poor man can share their space and food, made him almost an icon in Hindi cinema. The symbolism of the hero and a mongrel sharing the sidewalk, made people cry where

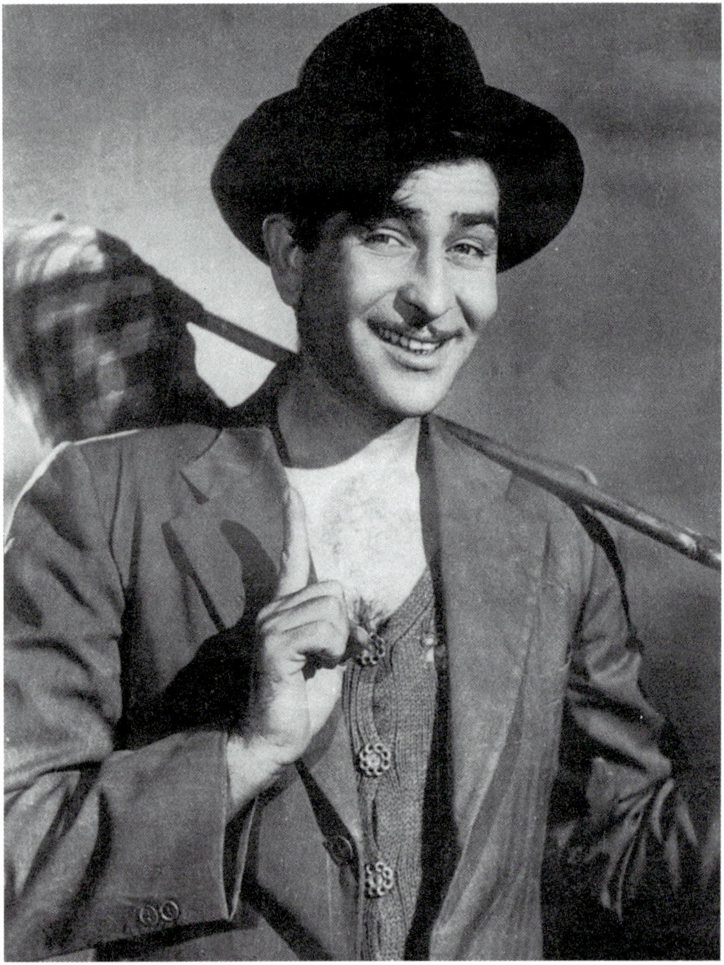

Raj Kapoor wanted them to and he had the entire country eating out of his hands.

In the post-independence era, the country required large gulps of emotional sentimentality and Raj Kapoor had correctly felt the pulse of his audiences. Not too much taxing of the brain, good music, simple themes which went straight to the heart and he had not only a hit film on his hands but one which in its own insidious way makes a statement even in this age of computers. His *'Ramaiyavastavaiya .... maine dil tujhko diya'* suggested once more that it required only love to change the social order and bring it to rights.

Interestingly, *Shri 420* was saying all this in the guise of comedy — it remains one of the better comedies in Hindi films. The scenes where he woos Nargis with a cup of tea but brazenly asks her to pay for it because he has only Rs.100 notes, remains a scene where in pure RK tradition, you have to laugh and cry at the same time. The number *'Pyar hua ikrar hua hai'* became an anthem, the scene where the two leading actors walk in the rain sharing an umbrella – is a never-to-be-forgotten visual.

The happy-go-lucky tramp then appeared in *Anari,* and inspired *Jis Desh Mein Ganga Behti Hai,* where Raj Kapoor as the simple

Pran and Raj Kapoor in Jis Desh Mein Ganga Behti Hai

villager sets out to reform dacoits. He believes that they are actually socialists who are balancing the world by making the rich a little poorer and the poor a little richer till he discovers their unnecessary violence. *Chhalia* again showed Raj Kapoor as the reformer — this time around seeking to build a spirit of unity between the Hindus and Muslims. This theme was continued in *Henna, Abdullah* and *Khan Dost.*

Three generations of the Kapoor family, Prithviraj Kapoor, Raj Kapoor and Randhir Kapoor acted together for the first time in Kal Aaj Aur Kal

Sangam was Raj Kapoor's first colour film dealing with the most popular of Hindi film themes – the love triangle. Since it was Raj Kapoor, there had to be a moral inherent even here. The alternation between tradition and modernity, between the sanctity of marriage and the ideals of friendship and sacrifice, as well as love for one's country, all showcased Raj Kapoor the idealist at his very best.

Kal Aaj Aur Kal — an ambitious film showing three generations represented by Randhir Kapoor, Raj Kapoor and Prithviraj Kapoor was lapped up by audiences, once again as a RK product. Raj Kapoor plays the present generation sandwiched between the traditions of the past and the desires of the future generation. As he tries to maintain a balance between grandfather and grandson, he enacts a role that becomes both comic and a little priest-like as he hammers across the relative virtues of both the past and the future generations.

Mandakini in Ram Teri Ganga Maili

The role of the tramp culminated in his biographical blockbuster *Mera Naam Joker,* an ambitious project by any standards. It was a long film with two intervals, took six years to make and was divided into three stories. Raj Kapoor put everything he possessed into this film, both financially and emotionally. And played the title role himself. The lovable tramp was submerged into the gallant joker who keeps laughing at life's injustices, while his heart bleeds. Audiences knew they were watching something real here. Yet the film failed. Raj Kapoor was broken. He couldn't believe that his midas touch had deserted him this time. *Joker* remains the only film made by Raj Kapoor that bombed at the box office.

After this he made a quickie *Bobby*, which became an instant hit. So did his subsequent films. But now Raj Kapoor had started taking recourse to sensuality and all films like *Satyam Shivam Sundaram, Ram Teri..., Bobby* played to the gallery, in terms of exposing the female body. But again before anyone could point fingers at this, they had to admit that *Satyam Shivam* had a beautiful theme too — and in *Ram Teri Ganga Maili,* his *Ganga* was the epitome of all that is good and pure in this country. Just as his tramp image ended in *Joker*, his vision of what a beautiful woman represents culminated in *Ganga*. In *Prem Rog* he was making a conscious statement about liberating women and all these films succeeded; for from this filmmaker people expected some social message too.

CHAPTER SIX

The Actor

Once Raj Kapoor was present at a perfomance by Topol (the actor in *Fiddler on the Roof*). When the play ended and the applause died down, Topol announced, "Ladies and gentlemen, there is a misconception that I am Israel's most popular actor. That's wrong. I am the second most popular man, the first being Raj Kapoor of India, who is present here with us today." He then called Raj Kapoor to the stage to a standing ovation.

Everyone knew Raj Kapoor and this popularity, both at home and abroad, can be attributed to his ability to appeal both to the head and the heart at once. Raj Kapoor as an actor, had a fan following in India which could cause riots when he went out in public. The mobility of his face, the deep blue eyes which could portray both love and sadness with equal depth, the fine skin and the variety of expressions which crossed his face, made him adorable, the darling of the Indian masses. The audiences identified with him at an almost psychological level. He was at once the joker, the tramp, the clown and the romantic.

Only Raj Kapoor had the capacity to convey grief with a smile. In those days, the Indian audience was divided into two factions — the Dilip Kumar fans who loved his tragic intensity, and the Raj Kapoor loyalists who considered him the greater actor. "Can Dilip Kumar convey tragedy while smiling" they would ask unanswerably. Dilip was the larger-than-life tragedy

The gallant joker, who laughed, while his heart bled

king, while Raj modelled himself on the underdog, the street mongrel, the lovable homeless tramp who transformed the society around him through love.

Nanda remembers, "His face could express the tiniest of nuances with ease. If he was jealous, there would be a smirk on his face. If he was sad, his eyes reflected it immediately. I consider him the finest actor we have, along with Dilip Kumar."

In Mehboob's Andaz, *Nargis, Raj Kapoor and Dilip Kumar.*

Raj Kapoor the director never intruded on Raj Kapoor the actor when he did outside films. His heroine Waheeda Rehman recalls, "When we were shooting for *Ek Dil Sau Afsane* and later for *Teesri Kasam*, I would often feel that some things were not right and must be changed. But he would merely say 'I am not the director here, I'm only the actor and will do just as I am told!' But even in those days, he was full of great ideas for his own films and talked about making *Henna* and *Satyam Shivam Sundaram*."

With Nargis in Jagte Raho

"I," says Nanda, "realised what a good actor he was when I played his wife in *Aashiq*. In one scene, I had to confront him and Padmini saying, 'Whatever you are doing, do it in front of me!' I was merely a teenager then, and very nervous about firing these two established seniors. But Raj Kapoor came up to me and said 'Nanda, *yeh tumhara scene hai.* I know you are going to do it well.' And he insisted that director Hrishikesh Mukherji keep the camera on me. I realised how much confidence he had in himself as an actor to give up the scene to a co-star so completely"

Chapter Seven

The Filmmaker

That he was a filmmaker first and an actor later cannot be doubted. He himself said, "My becoming an actor was an accident, I have always wanted to be a filmmaker." As a filmmaker, Raj Kapoor's USP was also perhaps his greatest flaw. For, unlike his peers Guru Dutt, Mehboob Khan or Bimal Roy, Raj Kapoor had no clearly defined philosophy in his films, except perhaps the philosophy of love. Though his films always had a social message, it was a slightly unrealistic and slightly superficial one. He believed that the inequalities in society could be resolved by a romantic optimism and never really delved deeply into them.

He saw himself firstly as an entertainer and that's what he was as a filmmaker — a supreme entertainer. His tendency to romanticise poverty, cruelty, inequality showed an evasiveness as a filmmaker. He used these issues as a peg for his films but they remained just pegs. There were no real solutions offered by him. He believed that people came to the cinema to be entertained and that's what he was doing — entertaining them. He did not consider cinema

In 1964, while shooting for Sangam *in Ooty*

Radhu Karmakar, Raj Kapoor's cinematographer, 1979

an intellectual medium, yet believed that it could become the medium of change. But through emotionalism and sentimentality. And that is the level at which his films worked best.

Despite his almost naïve romanticism, he was not only considered the greatest entertainer by his audiences but in terms of box office figures, it was seen that he was perhaps the only filmmaker whose distributors remained with him throughout his life and career. No mean achievement in the fluctuating world of films! Filmmaker Shyam Benegal, the master of realistic cinema, once analysed Raj Kapoor's work with: "His probing (of issues) never quite takes on radical dimensions, remaining satisfied with platitudinous happy endings."

In Raj Kapoor's films, women are often treated as the focal points as seen in *Barsaat, Sangam, Mera Naam Joker, Bobby, Satyam Shivam Sundaram, Ram Teri Ganga Maili* and *Prem Rog*. But his women were still passive beings, either waiting for their man *(Barsaat),* sacrificing themselves (*Sangam*) or becoming victims of society *(Ram Teri Ganga Maili* and *Prem Rog)*. In *Mera Naam Joker,* the women became the temptresses who seduced the poor hero. In *Bobby,* the heroine was the epitome of youthful sex appeal for whom the hero would surmount any obstacle. Despite that, these women always suffered more or less in silence or symbolised the need to change the norms of society.

Raj Kapoor often spoke of how women in India were deified as 'Mata' (mother) on the one hand and ill treated on the other. According to him, women should be put on a pedestal. Only, his pedestal suggested a superwoman who had no need for self-gratification; that was the man's prerogative. The woman was higher than that. She was the 'Devi' who transcended all mundane desires. His love for women dressed in white, in his personal life, perhaps reflected this attitude.

Satyam Shivam Sundaram was actually an expression of Raj Kapoor's recurrent motif — the supremacy of inner beauty over physical beauty. In his films, he wanted to keep proving that inner beauty was more fascinating. But somewhere down the line, his fascination for the female body overshadowed and contradicted his ideal. And during the course of his film making, he did became known for his unnecessary exploitation of the female form. His first film *Aag* dealt with this theme, so did *Satyam, Shivam, Sundaram*.

Applying make-up on Zeenat Aman in Satyam Shivam Sundaram

Many saw his voyeurism, his obsession with the female form as "the carnality of a schoolboy". But beyond this criticism, he remained forever the romantic optimist, attributing it to the atmosphere of the post-independence years. "We began our work in an age of optimism. The Republic was new, and the rulers were new to leadership," he explained once.

His films can be considered 'masala' films of the best kind; films which had tried and tested themes, loads of emotionalism and sentimentality, loads of traditions rooted in our culture, loads of relationships based on the Indian value system and magnificent music. And he spared no efforts in achieving this. He worked at a leisurely pace sparing no costs. This was helped by the fact that he had a studio of his own. Perhaps he'd constructed the studio because it suited his temperament to not have time limits and finances dictate his way of working.

Directing Simi Garewal in Mera Naam Joker

Simi Garewal recalls during the making of *Mera Naam Joker*, "His whole scale was very big and the time element was never important. He never had that *jaldi kaam khatam karo* attitude like other people. He had a studio at his disposal so he could take his time over shooting. Everything was done in a rather leisurely manner. And he was a perfectionist."

"For example, in *Mera Naam Joker,* when we'd go location hunting, the whole team would travel together. We finally reached a place in Mysore, which had a little river — that's where Chintu and I did the famous river scene. It seemed fine to me. But he told his crew 'alright, make it'. I didn't know what 'make it' meant. We came back four days later to shoot and the place looked completely transformed. The crew had sprayed the leaves, made them greener, added some darker red colours, spruced up the whole place and it really looked different. This was the first time I had ever seen anyone playing with nature and it really struck me."

"Another incident also happened in Mysore, during the last *alaap* of the song *Teetar ke do aage teetar...* He wanted the teacher to lead this whole group of students over the mountain, with a fabulous sunset at the back. Every single day, I would do this whole run up the hill with all these kids following me — there'd be generator trucks being moved, lights being moved, everything would be set up. And then he would say, '*Haan theek hai..... kal karenge*!' because he wasn't happy with the sunset! This went on for fourteen days until he got the perfect sunset he wanted."

"He would also shoot a lot of footage. In the Padmini episode, he

Directing Rishi Kapoor and Dimple Kapadia in Bobby

shot a lakh-and-a-half feet of footage. People didn't do that. I was working simultaneously with Satyajit Ray, who was so precise and abstemious with his footage that the maximum he'd exposed for the full film was thirty thousand feet. That was quite a contrast and it was quite interesting to compare the two."

"That was Rajji's working style. He made you feel good — that

Nanda and Padmini Kolhapure in Prem Rog

was something I learnt from him. If you are feeling good about yourself, your voice opens up, you talk well, you emote confidently. He would pamper the artiste a lot and make you really feel like a queen. When you worked with him, you became part of the RK family."

"I remember, at that time when we went to Pune for shootings, his farmhouse wasn't really done up. The entire unit, including me, would be sleeping on bags spread out on the terrace. I had never done this sort of thing before. I remember how much fun we had going over to someone else's mattress and sitting and chatting for long hours. It was a memorable time. It had never happened before and can never happen again."

Nanda looks back upon her experiences with him fondly: "He was a fine filmmaker. When he was directing me in *Prem Rog*, I had just three scenes in the film but the way he crafted them allowed me ample scope to show my talent. It used to be a joy to watch him act out each character's scenes in their individual styles. He gave each artiste, however big or small, the same love and respect. In fact, the way he pampered his artistes was very heartwarming. He made a fantastic host both as a producer and at his parties. The warmth with which he treated you made you feel alien in other environments. If the press visited his sets during *Prem Rog*, he would tell them – these young people (Rishi Kapoor and Padmini Kolhapure) are not my stars. My stars are Shammi Kapoor, Tanuja, Nanda.' His love really reached out to all of us."

Chapter Eight

The Musician

Despite his permanent musical team comprising Shankar-Jaikishan, lyricists Shailendra and Hasrat Jaipuri and singer Mukesh, it was Raj Kapoor himself whose stamp pervades all his music. He had a great ear for music, an innate sense of rhythm and could play most musical instruments by ear. His favourites were the *dholak* and the *tabla*. His favourite ragas were Bhairavi, Shivranjani, Pahari, Malkauns and Darbari.

Raj Kapoor's song sittings were famous. He loved to listen to tunes, to prune and trim the compositions, to correct the singers. While his lyricists wrote, he fine tuned the lyrics, and while the composers composed, he perfected the compositions to suit his taste.

Till date, the music of all his films remains immensely popular and has Raj Kapoor's signature indelibly on it. One just hears a bar of his music and can identify it as a composition from RK Films. Lata Mangeshkar reiterated this at a function to celebrate *Ram Teri Ganga Maili*. She said, "The music of RK Films may have been

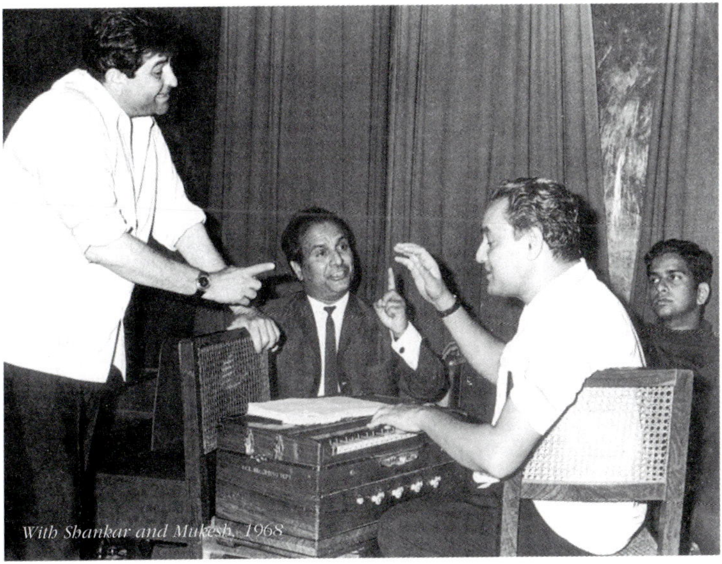

With Shankar and Mukesh, 1968

attributed to Shankar-Jaikishan, then Laxmikant-Pyarelal and then Ravindra Jain. But I, as the singer who has sung for his productions from *Barsaat* onwards, can vouch for the fact that all of RK music is in the ultimate analysis Raj Kapoor's own creation."

He admitted, "From the earliest days, I have been interested in music. In fact, my first ambition was to be a music director. I even sang in my earlier films like *Chitchor*, *Chitor Vijay*, *Jail Yatra* and

Making music in 1970

Gopinath. When words fail, it is music that conveys much more than all words put together." And he more than executed this in his song picturisations.

In his films, the songs stand out not as mere reliefs from the narrative or as intrusions, but are important cogs which move the story forward. Like his peers Bimal Roy and Guru Dutt, he gave as much importance to the execution of a song as to a scene.

Awaara

The songs were often important expressions of emotions which could not be conveyed through dialogues.

Raj Kapoor's songs could even be considered the real triggers of social change, even more than the films themselves. The lyrics had real substance. For him, the songs were truly not only audio but audio-visual. He *saw* music as it were; and only when he could see visually how the song could be filmed, did he okay its recording. His use of elaborate sets, of light and shade to convey sombreness and technicolour to project joy, were all part of his visual perception. He was so closely associated with his music that in *Jagte Raho,* when the song *'Zindagi khwab hai'* was picturised on Motilal rather than on Raj himself, the public was bewildered.

The songs were always recorded first and it is said that his tunes were composed even before the lyrics were written. But there were interesting exceptions like *Boot Polish* and *Jis Desh Mein Ganga Behti Hai.* Initially, there were going to be no songs in

Boot Polish, directed by Prakash Arora under the RK banner (though the Raj Kapoor touch is blatantly evident in the film). But after viewing the film, Raj Kapoor decided it needed songs. And for the first time in his production, songs were written, composed and situations created for them after the whole film was complete! So exquisite are the songs of *Boot Polish* and so beautifully interwoven into the film that no one would guess that a *'Chali*

The magic team (left to right) Dattaram, Om Prakash Mehra, Shankar, Hasrat Jaipuri, Raj Kapoor, Mukesh (at the harmonium), Raja Nawathe, Jaikishen and Shailendra

kaun se desh gujariya tu sajh dhajh ke', or *'John chacha tum kitne acche'*, or *'Nanhe munne bache teri muthi main kya hai'*, were not part of the original script.

In *Jis Desh Mein Ganga Behti Hai*, Shankar did not want to compose at all, as dacoity was hardly the subject musicals were made of! So Raj Kapoor got the songs written first, and when Shankar realised the beauty of the lyrics, he composed the music. And these songs ultimately touched listeners where it hurt the most. They became almost anthems, to be sung at every independence day ceremony — numbers like *'Aa ab laut chalen'* and *'Jis desh main ganga behti hai'*.

As a filmmaker, Raj Kapoor often took recourse to a song to introduce his character — a rather interesting and entertaining introduction device. For example, his *'Mera joota hai Japani yeh patloon Inglistani ... phir bhi dil hai Hindustani'* established the hero's character in *Shri 420*. *'Awara hoon... ya gardish main hoon aasman ka tara hoon'* establishes the identity of the tramp in *Awara*. This ploy allowed the song as much importance as an opening scene. The singularly hummable numbers were known to the audiences by heart and they watched his films again and again, adoring the lovable tramp happily dancing through the streets.

And, of course, Raj Kapoor's musical genius found enough situations for utterly melodious romantic numbers like *'Han maine pyar kiya, hai hai kya zulm kiya…, hum bhi hain, tum bhi ho'.* He himself analysed, "My subject always suggested to me a particular kind of musical style unerringly — the style that would work out audio-visually right in the final unfolding of the film."

It is said that even the lyrics of his songs were often sourced from his own life's experiences. Once he and Nargis were travelling by

Raj Kapoor with Lata Mangeshkar

Raj Kapoor with Rajendra Kumar and Vyajantimala in Sangam

train and they had a tiff. She got off the train and left. He turned to his companion saying "Khan *saab, dekho na, chhod gaye balam, akela chhod gaye!"* This was the germ of that classic number.

Again, during the making of *Bobby* he was talking on the phone with Simi Garewal, who was grooming the young Dimple for her film debut. At something she said he responded, *"Tum jhoot bol rahi ho."* Simi, taken aback, replied, "I'm not lying, why should I?" But he insisted, *"Nahin, tum jhooth bol rahi ho— tumhe kaala kauwa kaate ga!"* That was the genesis of *'Jhooth bole kauwa kaate....'!*

Raj Kapoor greatly admired Lata Mangeshkar and his relationship with her remained turbulent, with the lady often taking umbrage when things did not go her way. But he always made it a point to make up with her. He just could not visualise his films without her singing.

Lata Mangeshkar's tiff with him when she had to sing *'Main ka karoon Ram mujhe buddha mil gaya'* in *Sangam*, has become legendary. She objected to the double meaning in the lyrics. But Raj Kapoor uncompromisingly insisted the song be sung as it is and by her alone. Though the lady was upset, the recording was done. Raj was not past cajoling, persuading and making everything subservient to the major goal of fulfilling his cinematic vision.

Later, in his biggest fiasco, *Mera Naam Joker*, it was Asha Bhonsle who sang for him, as in *'Kahin daag na lag jaaye'*. But when the film failed, it was partly attributed to Lata Mangeshkar's absence from the film and when she reappeared in the RK produced *Bobby*, it's success was also attributed to her presence.

Chapter Nine

The Man

One could call him the eternal Sagittarian; full of optimism, a dreamer, shooting arrows at the stars, hoping one would fall into his hands....He dreamt huge dreams and sold dreams to his audiences. His generosity is legendary. He was full of contradictions — loving, very affectionate but often malicious and harsh; and willing to go to any lengths to make his films. He had no qualms about apologising to anyone if he was required back in the RK fold. His was an odd juxtaposition of the missionary and the star

— a humility along with an innate arrogance which has become a Kapoor trademark.

In 1946, at the age of 22, he was married to Krishna, his father's cousin. When Nargis came into his life, he was already married and the father of one child. With this new relationship, his marriage became increasingly turbulent. Krishna even left home with the kids to go to her father's house in Jabalpur. But Krishna was given full support by her in-laws and was called back. So intense was his relationship with Nargis that Raj Kapoor never imagined that anything could spoil it. But Nargis realised that she couldn't go on — she wanted marriage.

It is said that she even approached Morarji Desai, then Home Minister, for permission to marry the already married Raj, but was refused. Neither could she see Raj Kapoor leaving his children and family to marry her. He cared too much for his family and for the norms of society to really flout them, but in his naïve trustworthiness he hoped and perhaps expected, Nargis to understand. It was around this time that she was offered *Mother India* by Mehboob Khan. Here she met Sunil Dutt and after an incident where he saved her life when a set caught fire, she agreed to marry him.

Raj Kapoor and Nargis

Yet, the Raj Kapoor-Nargis romance remains one of the more popular off-screen and on- screen romances the Hindi film world has seen. There was a spiritual, exalted quality about their love and audiences identified with this. They did 16 films together and audiences adored them. The pair was looked upon with indulgence and affection and everyone accepted them both as a couple.

When Nargis left him, Raj Kapoor was broken. He couldn't come to terms with the fact that she was no longer a part of his life and, more importantly, his films. The period when she left was one of his worst phases. He was difficult, moody, used to cry, was abusive and often uncontrollable. Friends used to advise him to take physical exercise, go swimming, get away from the familiar surroundings to get her out of his system, but to no avail.

Raj Kapoor had cast Nargis in his first film *Aag* but it was in *Barsaat* that they seemed to discover each other. After that they became a pair to be watched out for. Their involvement was there for all to see. On screen their love scenes crackled with an intensity which made for high drama.

In true celluloid spirit, Nargis' last film with him was *Jagte Raho* in which she played a small cameo, coming in only in the last scene, and shown as the person who is finally able to quench the poor protagonist's thirst. Very poignant. Audiences hated it. They wanted to see the romantic Raj-Nargis pair. They felt cheated to see her in this benevolent *avatar.* The film didn't do well in it's first run. But it seemed like poetic justice to all who knew them closely. For this was their final film together and what better way to say goodbye?

His "soft corners" for his later-day heroines like Padmini and Vyjantimala too created ripples. Krishna once again had occasion to leave home during his Vyjanti phase. But this didn't last long and the family was together again. In later life, Raj Kapoor became very close to his wife Krishna. Even earlier insiders say that he never let her feel the want of anything as a wife. It might be truer to say that Raj Kapoor loved films so much that he loved everything that went with them — his cast, his crew, his workers, his spot boys, just everyone and this included his heroines too.

Nimmi recalls that during the shooting of *Barsaat,* he was so concerned about his workers that whenever there was night shooting, he would keep talking to the lightboys who sat near the roof of the studio on wooden planks, in order to keep them alert and in good humour. His workers all adored him for his affection. "On night shoots, there'd appear baskets of fruits which were peeled and cut and everyone was fed, not just the stars but the workers too; there'd be glasses of *lassi* going around, with that kind of atmosphere why wouldn't anyone give their best to him?"

As a father, Raj Kapoor adored his children. He was particularly close to his daughters Ritu and Rima as well as to his sons Daboo (Randhir) and Chimpu (Rajeev Kapoor). But Neetu Singh, his daughter-in-law, laughs as she reveals: "Chintu (Rishi), my husband, used to be petrified of him for some reason. And as if that wasn't enough, papa (Rajji) too was scared of Chintu. Chintu would call me and ask, 'Papa has come, what is he saying'. And papa would refer to him as *badasaab* and say to me '*badasaab aa gaya, kya kar raha hai badasaab?* Would he like me to do something for him? Would he like this? Take some *mithai* for him.' He would give me things to give him but they'd avoid talking to each other for some reason."

Neetu Singh, who married Rishi Kapoor in 1980, lived with her in-laws in Chembur for the first year of her marriage and fell absolutely in love with her father-in-law. "He was so perceptive, he could look at your face and gauge what you were thinking. There were times when I'd be terribly hurt and nobody would understand but he'd call me and say 'this is what is happening, I

A man of varied tastes

know' and I'd burst into tears. You just had to sit with him to feel his affection and you would learn a lot. He would talk about life and its experiences and you were always the wiser for having listened to him. He never gave lectures, just talked about everything under the sun."

"He adored his grandchildren. He named my son Ranbir after himself and my daughter Riddhima. Both my daughter and Kareena were born within a week of each other during the Ganpati festival and he was very moved. He would say, '*meri do shakti aa gayi*'. When we shifted residence to Pali Hill, my children would run to be with their grandparents as soon as they got a day off. His pet name for Ranbir was 'Gonglu' and if I ever scolded him, he would ring up papaji and complain to him about me and papa would scold me for scolding him! The kids adored him."

His contradictions were as huge as his personality. He loved to be surrounded by people, cared for his cast and crew as if they were family. Yet he could be as selfish as he was benevolent, as egoistic as he was friendly. He had an innate arrogance which kept people in awe of him. He loved to eat and drink and each day he would take whoever was with him at the time, to Geeta Bhavan, a small Udipi restaurant in Chembur, to eat his favourite *idlis* and *vadas*.

"He considered himself almost infallible" says Chandru Hingorani, brother of filmmaker Arjun Hingorani. He could be very selfish and arrogant but was so affectionate too, that one just couldn't stay away from him. We used to fight and make up all the time. I joined him as an assistant in 1953 but became friends with him about six years later. Till his *Joker* flopped, he saw himself as supreme. He couldn't believe he could do anything wrong. But after *Joker*, he was broken. He never recovered despite the success of *Bobby* and *Ram Teri Ganga Maili*.

Raj Kapoor and Mukesh, 1973

Simi recalls his loving care during *Mera Naam Joker.* "He loved his unit. Every hour that we passed with him, whether it was travelling together or eating together, was fun. Once we were travelling by train, after a lovely shoot in Simla. When we reached Solan, he got out, went into the train's kitchen, and announced, 'I am going to make my eggs Monte Carlo'."

"His recipe was to break an egg over a slice of bread and fry it. He must have made about 200 eggs that day, not only for our team but also for fellow travellers on the train. They couldn't believe that here was filmstar Raj Kapoor making eggs for them. He fed his unit, loved them, looked after them. When we reached Delhi he said, 'Now you people go to your hotel, *main kuch khaas cheez lane ja raha hoon'*. He went to Chandni Chowk and bought this unbelievable *puri-aloo*. Then he came and delivered this personally to everybody. He did such things out of sheer affection."

People close to him say that he had this habit of getting drunk and speaking his mind. But the fact was that he was never really drunk. He just pretended to be drunk so that he could speak the unpalatable truth and tell someone what he thought of him in the plainest terms. Simi corroborates, "Yes, he was never really drunk. He knew what he was saying. But since he could not say it when he was sober, he pretended to be drunk and got it off his chest. I used to get very upset when he did this. And whenever I saw him get into this mood, I would run miles away from him."

"He had his eccentricities but they were more fun than anything else," recalls Simi. "I remember the fun times with him. He was a late riser and it was a pain and a nuisance for him to get up early. Once, while shooting in Darjeeling, I don't know what made him get up as early as 4 or 5 in the morning and start banging on everybody's door shouting in his affectionate way *'sote rehte ho, kaam karo*, the sun is rising, it's a perfect day'. We all got ready with costumes, make-up, etc. and went to his room – only to find that his majesty had gone back to sleep!"

Waheeda Rehman laughingly recounts, "When we were cast in *Ek Dil Sau Afsane*, I arrived on the set at the required time, but he would come very late. For a nine o'clock shift, he would turn up at 2 pm. The director felt sorry for me and one day said, 'Do not leave your house till I call and inform you that Rajji has arrived.' Later that day, when the director jokingly asked what time he could be expected tomorrow, Rajji promptly replied, 'At seven'. I added, 'Do you mean seven in the morning or in the evening?' He said, 'You just wait and watch.' The next day, though ready, I did not go to the set. Suddenly I got a frantic call from the director, 'Waheedaji, come soon, Rajji arrived here at a quarter to seven!' He loved doing things like that."

Raj Kapoor was one of the few people in the industry who remained loyal to those who had helped him. For example, whenever he was being applauded, he never forgot to mention Kidar Sharma, his mentor, teacher and the first filmmaker to cast him as hero. It did not make him feel small to acknowledge Sharma's contribution in his life. After *Neelkamal*, Raj Kapoor set out on his own and became probably better known than his guru.

Raj Kapoor at his farm 1967

Kidar Sharma once called him to act opposite a new girl in his film *Bawre Nain.* The girl was Geeta Bali, a fledgling, while Raj Kapoor was an established star by the time. But Kidar Sharma knew the girl's incredible talent though Raj Kapoor didn't. Raj responded at once to his director's call, merely saying "Sharmaji, I hope you are casting someone who is equal to me in calibre?" Kidar Sharma replied, "What calibre are you talking about?"

When shooting started, Raj Kapoor was flabbergasted by the girl's incredible screen presence and had to admit that she was astounding. Sheepishly he took the director aside and said, "Sharmaji, please don't take close ups of us together, this girl eats up the screen!" The girl later became his younger brother Shammi Kapoor's wife.

A respect for elders and gratitude for those who had helped him were Raj Kapoor's endearing characteristics. But he also had a typically chauvinistic attitude towards women – they must remain

With star brother Shammi Kapoor (extreme left) renowned Kathak dancer Sitara Devi, and film star Rajendra Kumar, 1970

at home; at least the Raj Kapoor women must. Neetu remembers, "The *holi* revelries at RK were always fun. Family and friends would come, there was singing and dancing, and everyone was dumped into the pool, but not the women. Women played with dry colours and papa saw to it that no one misbehaved with the ladies."

While his three sons Randhir, Rishi and Rajeev joined films, his two daughters, Rima and Rita have been successfully married off. His own wife Krishna always remained in the background. So much so that even today, thirteen years after his death, when a well known TV series commemorated his life and work and spoke to his whole family, Krishna refused to be interviewed. That his elder son Randhir's daughters, Karisma and Kareena have become high profile filmstars was seen initially as an aberration even leading to a split in the Randhir-Babita marriage. While both Randhir and Rishi married established filmstars, they had to give up their careers in order to be Kapoor *bahus.*

Raj Kapoor believed in lasting relationships and this was seen in the cohesiveness of his crew in RK Productions too. Radhu Karmakar the cameraman who shot *Awara,* remained with Raj Kapoor till he died and shot his last film *Ram Teri Ganga Maili* as well as *Henna* after Rajji's death. The music duo Shankar-Jaikishan remained with him till the latter's death in 1970. And, he always maintained that he had on tape enough Shankar-Jaikishan melodies to last all RK films. Shailendra and Hasrat Jaipuri wrote for him till their respective deaths and writers V.P.Sathe and K.A.Abbas remained with him for decades.

Chandru Hingorani reveals, "Once, after a fight, I did not speak to him for five years. But he kept sending me messages to meet him. One day, in 1985, a common friend forced me to visit Raj Kapoor who immediately said, *'Arre mere bhai...* I am now dying. Don't quarrel with me any more!' His health was bad, his asthma had worsened and he had quit smoking by that time."

"His simplicity was astounding in such a big star. His habits were sparse. Each time he went abroad, he would buy me these expensive shoes from Bally's, a famous Swiss brand. Once, while shopping with Rajendra Kumar, the latter asked why he wasn't buying these shoes for himself. He said, 'I can't afford such luxuries! These are for Prince.' He always called me Prince because though I was always short of money, my tastes were royal!"

"During the film festival in Delhi, as I forgot my shaving kit and was going out to buy a razor, he said, 'Are you crazy, use mine!' I actually shared his shaving kit for the two weeks we were there.

At cricket—his favourite sport

He was so down to earth. If he was fond of you, he would go to any lengths for you. If I wanted to holiday abroad, he would buy me a return ticket and give me *carte blanche* to spend as much money as I needed!"

Nimmi agrees, "I was his *raakhi* sister from the start and he gave so much importance to this relationship. Once, on *raksha bandhan* day, I got delayed. On entering his house, I overheard him tell his wife, '*Arre Nimmi ab tak kyon nahin aayi, phone karke dekho kahin tabiyat to kharaaab nahin hai?*' His affection was phenomenal, he always addressed me as *beheniya* and he never

forgot to invite me to every function in his house!"

Raj Kapoor was not merely a man, nor merely a filmmaker — he was an entire lifestyle. Everything surrounding him was larger than life — his films, his affairs, his affections, his eccentricities, his dreams, even his losses (he never quite recovered from the huge loss incurred by *Mera Naam Joker*, and it is said that he was scheduled to meet the President in Delhi to ask for a one-time tax amnesty, when he collapsed at the function where he was being honoured with the Dadasaheb Phalke award) his parties, his mahurats and his holi revelries. This festival of colours was celebrated at RK as a tradition. Everyone waited to be invited to it and only then could he/she be said to have "arrived" in true Hindi-film-style!

At Loni, his farm near Pune, he was a much loved figure. While 'home' was wife Krishna's domain, Loni and RK Studio was his, and he was inordinately proud of inviting people there and playing host. The villagers at Loni adored him and he'd sit with them on a cot and listen to their problems. Once they complained that there was no school nearby and Raj Kapoor is said to have built one for them.

The 35th National Film Festival award presentation ceremony in New Delhi, Raj Kapoor got the Dada Saheb Phalke Award, May 2, 1988

"He would take the whole family to the farm," says Neetu, "and we were made to relax while papa took over the kitchen. He was a fabulous cook and could cook everything. But he especially made exotic pastas and excellent *gobi,* his favourite vegetable. It's a misconception that he loved to eat. He loved to see food and to feed people, but hardly ate himself. Even at home in Chembur, he would serve everyone but himself ate only a *khurjaon* (what Simi referred to as eggs Monte Carlo) a Peshawari way of making eggs — or have something simple like *pao* and *chai*. In the evening, he'd go to Geeta Bhavan to eat *idlis* but lunch was just a *khurjaon*.

"He would order these special Alphonso mangoes and place one in your hand, saying 'Cut it and eat it, it's very tasty'. There used to be boxes of chocolates in his room and his grandchildren were called in – *'salaam karo'* he'd say, and then give them chocolates. This was a ritual he followed and the kids always fell for it." Everything he did had that special Raj Kapoor touch to it.

Even his death, when it came, was spectacular. He collapsed during the ceremony when the Dadasaheb Phalke Award was being conferred upon him by the President. He was rushed in the President's ambulance to the All India Medical Institute in Delhi. His last words as he was being carried on the stretcher were to his wife "Krishna, I'm going, I'm going, goodbye, goodbye!"

Interesting Facts

- Raj Kapoor was allergic to air travel, disliked heights in general, always slept on the floor and usually did not get up before mid-day.

- Raj Kapoor was always urging Dilip Kumar to get married. When he finally did marry Saira Banu, Raj Kapoor was so thrilled that he danced Punjabi-style with the *baraatis!* Both Raj Kapoor and Dilip Kumar hailed from Peshawar and enjoyed ragging each other.

- Raj Kapoor was the youngest of the Dev/ Dilip/ Raj triumvirate.

- He thought he may have been a Buddhist monk in a previous incarnation as a marked leaning towards the spiritual managed to creep into every film he made.

- He was very close to his parents and could never be overawed by them as they were only 16 (mother) and 18 (father) years older than him.

- Each time wife Krishna visited RK Studios, he would proudly show her around, playing the host and treating her like a loved guest.

- Raj Kapoor loved flowers, especially *mogras.*

- Raj Kapoor liked women to wear white. Nargis always wore white after she became friendly with him.

- Hrishikesh Mukherji wrote his film *Anand* initially with Raj Kapoor in mind. The two shared a great deal of affection and Raj called Hrishida 'Babu moshai' all his life.

- After Nargis married Sunil Dutt, she met Raj Kapoor at the ladies *sangeet* party organised for Rishi Kapoor's wedding. The next year, in 1981, she died of cancer.

Filmography

R K Films

1948 Aag
1949 Barsaat
1951 Awara
1953 Aah
1954 Boot Polish
1955 Shree 420
1956 Jagte Raho
1957 Ab Dilli Door Nahin
1960 Jis Desh Mein Ganga Behti Hai
1964 Sangam
1971 Mera Naam Joker
1971 Kal Aaj Aur kal
1973 Bobby
1975 Dharam Karam
1978 Satyam Shivam Sundaram
1981 Biwi o Biwi
1982 Prem Rog
1985 Ram Teri Ganga Maili
1990 Henna

Outside Films

1935	Inquilab (Debaki Bose)
1943	Gauri (Kidar Sharma)
1943	Hamara Batt (M.I. Dharamsi)
1946	Valmiki (Bhalji Pendharkar)
1947	Chittor Vijay (Mohan Sinha)
1947	Dil Ki Rani (Mohan Sinha)
1947	Neel Kamal (Kidar Sharma)
1947	Jail Yatra (G. Jagirdar)
1948	Amar Prem (N.M. Kelkar)
1948	Gopinath (Mahesh Kaul)
1949	Andaz (Mehboob)
1949	Parivartan (N.R. Acharya)
1949	Sunhere Din (Satish Nigam)
1950	Bhanwra (G. Rakesh)
1950	Bawre Nain (Kidar Sharma)
1950	Dastaan (A.R. Kardar)
1050	Jan Pahchan (Fali Mistry)
1950	Sargam (P.L. Santoshi)
1952	Amber (Jayant Desai)
1952	Anhonee (K.A. Abbas)
1952	Ashiana (B. Trilochan)
1952	Dhoon (Kumar)
1953	Papi (Chandulal Shah)
1956	Chori Chori (Anant Thakur)
1957	Sharda (L.V. Prasad)

1958 Parvarish (S. Banerjee)
1958 Phir Subah Hogi (Ramesh Saigal)
1959 Anari (Hrishikesh Mukherjee)
1959 Char Dil Char Rahen (K.A. Abbas)
1959 Do Ustad (Tara Harish)
1959 Kanhaiya (Om Prakash)
1959 Main Nashe Mein Hoon (Naresh Saigal)
1960 Chhalia (Manmohan Desai)
1960 Shriman Satyawadi (S.M. Abbas)
1961 Nazrana (Shridhar)
1962 Aashiq (Hrishikesh Mukherjee)
1963 Dil Hi To Hai (P.L. Santoshi & C.L. Rawal)
1963 Ek Dil Sau Afsane (R.C. Talwar)
1964 Dulha Dulhan (Ravindra Dave)
1965 Teesri Kasam (Basu Bhattacharya)
1967 Around The World (Pachhi)
1967 Diwana (Mahesh Kaul)
1968 Sapnon Ka Saudagar (Mahesh Kaul)
1973 Mera Desh Mera Dharam (Dara Singh)
1975 Do Jasoos (Naresh Kumar)
1976 Khan Dost (Dulal Guha)
1977 Chandi Sona (Sanjay Khan)
1978 Naukri (Hrishikesh Mukherjee)
1980 Abdullah (Sanjay Khan)
1982 Gopichand Jasoos (Naresh Kumar)
1982 Vakil Baboo (Asit Sen)
1985 Char Mandali (C.L. Rawal)
1985 Umeed (Naresh Saigal)

RAJ KAPOOR'S
HANKAR JAIKISHAN
RAJ KAPOOR'S
MERA NAAM
JOKER
SHANKAR JAIKISHAN
KAL AAJ AUR KAL
RANDHIR KAPOOR
SHANKAR JAIKISHAN
J KAPOOR'S
SHREE 420
SHANKAR JAIKISHAN
RAJ KAPOOR'S
DHARAM KARAM
RANDHIR KAPOOR
R.D. BURMAN
RAJ KAPOOR'S
LAXMIKANT PYARELAL
RAJ KAPOOR'S
JIS DESH MEN GANGA BEHTI HAI
SHANKAR JAIKISHAN
RAJ KAPOOR'S
PREM ROG
RAJ KAPOOR'S
RAM teri GANGA maili